Cover by Bernard J Roberts
(Grandpa Roberts) 1983

FALLOWLANDS

(abridged)

POETRY

by

Bernard W Roberts

A copy of this book is also available at the
British Library

I

Published by
ninagiotti@btinternet.com
(abridged in hardback 2016)

first published 2011 paperback

isbn: 978-0-9930284-3-4 HARDBACK
isbn: 978-0-9538911-6-0 PAPERBACK

Also by the same author:

Adventures in Animaland isbn 0-9538911-3-5 or 978-0-95338911-1-5

Borealanus isbn 0-9538911-2-7 or 978-0-9538911-2-2

Café Deluxe isbn 0-9538911-4-6 or 978-0-9538911-2-2

Female Vortex (Civilization?) isbn 978-0-9930284-1-3

Female Vortex (Civilization?) isbn 2 978-0-9930284-2-7

George isbn 0-9538911-5-3 or 978-0-95389211-5-3

Intervention (stage) isbn 0-9538911-8-6 or 978-0-9538911-8-4

New Scripts (tv/film) isbn 0-9538911-7-8 or 978-0-9538911-7-7

On the Dole isbn 978-0-9930284-0-3

Rats isbn 0-9538911-0-0 or 978-0-9538911-0-8

Two Old Men Lost on a Mountain 0-9538911-9-4 or 978-0-9538911-9-1

A Working-Class Lament isbn 0-9538911-1-9 or 978-0-9538911-1-5

Synopses on Amazon UK books,
or order through any bookshop.

CONTENTS

NEW YEAR'S EVE
LIVERPOOL 1999

It was extensively reported by the media that, at midnight on the above date, catastrophic events would unfold; perhaps the world would end!

Under a lead-grey sky they walked,
a metamorphic crowd; few talked,
but most kept their eyes to the ground
as the millennium unwound
in and around Marks and Spencer's
and other high street dispensers
of consumer goods from other lands.
A mother, angry, restless hands,
pulled in opposite directions
like duplicated reflections
at the edge of angled plate-glass;
unemployed and yet working class.
Her kids, in expensive trainers,
kicked polystyrene containers
between steel and tubular poles
with fluorescent discount scrolls,
tinted mirrors, piped music,
veneer and plastic-coated brick.
But like the face paint on a clown
and smile that hides a forlorn frown,
the neon lights could not disguise
the shades of grey, despondent eyes.
In winter wraps they walked confused,
the well-off and poor interfused

by socialism and discontent:
Christmas behind and overspent.
On the corner of Basnett Street,
with frying pan and sandalled feet,
an ancient man clapped with relish,
the way a trained seal flaps for fish.
but this simpleton clapped with sense
enough to gain by false-pretence.
Sheltering in an arched doorway,
a young woman, untimely grey,
in curlers and ocelot coat
with matching love bites on her throat,
talked into the phone at her face,
her voice somewhere in outer space.
"*Who do you think you are?*" a long
thin man shouted at his sidelong
image with ladies' underwear.
"*Jesus Christ? Don't you soddin' stare*
at me like I'm a bag of scum."
Continuing to chew her gum,
the nearby girl with cellular
phone ignored the tall angular
man with the red and white striped hat.
"*Who do you think you're gawpin' at?*"
he shouted, nose against the glass:
"*Get out of my way, let me pass*".
Unaffected by calendar,
passers-by or the bystander
on the phone, he was middle-aged
and unwilling to be upstaged
by his double in the window
that followed him like a shadow.

"*Piss off*" he shouted to the glass
as an old woman tried to pass,
hump-backed, arthritic on a stick
with twisted feet, geriatric.
She dropped a shilling in the pan.
"*Thanks. luv*," the clapper-man began,
but the man in the hat karate-chopped
the air as two police mounts clopped
from a side street and into view,
trailing behind their residue.
Their mirrored image on the glass,
he watched the horseback riders pass
through pink and headless mannequins,
immodest but for sheets and pins.
"*Liverpool for the cup*," a youth,
in a paper hat and uncouth,
shouted from the Carnarvon door.
Striding, the tall man stood before
the grinning drunk, and face to face
with foreheads touching, sharing space,
the mad man shouted '*LIVERPOOL'*.
Original and man-made fool.
Upright on a bench, half asleep,
Jennifer Johnson, certified,
reprimanded her other side
with words beginning f and c.,
worldly possessions on her knee.
At the junction of Berry Street
a porter dragged a slab of meat
through an arch painted red and blue
while up the street next door but two

a Chinaman with blood-stained hands
scooped out the liver, heart and glands
and sliced the chicken into four;
decapitations on the floor.
Undercover and in disguise
with six days growth to empathize,
the plain-clothed cop strolled down the street
with strict instructions to defeat
the indistinguishable crook
who specializes in cheque book,
cash, credit card separation
and plastic bag confiscation.
But the felon, short in stature,
expert purse and wallet snatcher,
disappeared in the Church Street crowd.
With extra pockets for their swags
and Littlewoods' own branded bags,
mother and daughter moved between
the racks of nylon and sateen
blouses, bras and camiknickers,
stripping off the store's own stickers.
On the door to counter-attack,
dressed in official white and black,
security endomorphic,
replicated and endemic
but outnumbered and undermined
by the larceny in mankind.
The busy bars on Slater Street
spilled over, rocking to the beat
of fractured bones and displaced teeth.
In the shadows, a watchful thief.
Blanket-wrapped on a concrete seat

(with a notice marked 'trick or treat')
a beggar smoked cannabis resin,
while shaking his collection tin.
A street-singer standing below
the sign to Central Underground,
reaches high C in Figaro;
his empty trilby upside down.
Not more than two metres away,
in striped teeshirt and black beret,
a pavement artist on his knees
chalked a picture of Hercules,
one dimensional, muscle-bound;
culture for the homeward bound.
A financial demonstration
of mutual co-operation:
a son-et-lumiere presentation
leading to the subway station.
Up a verge on a roadside track,
with hands handcuffed behind his back
and head side-on metallic paint,
submissive under armed restraint:
truncheons, spray, bullet-proof jackets,
photofits, breathalyzer kits;
patrol cars with beacons spinning;
law and order underpinning
the mid-afternoon ring of steel
around the souped-up drugsmobile.
On an office block's second floor,
visible through an open door,
a woman bent double in tights
preparing for another night's
work, dying her hair coppertone

while taking bookings on the phone.
By the Cavern on a brick wall,
in multicoloured spray-can scrawl,
a phallic symbol ten feet wide
signed Anon of Merseyside.
The shoppers of Williamson Square
quietly breathed each other's air,
all fearful of the foreboding
that the year 2000 would bring
disaster and insanity
to civilized humanity.

JENNIFER JOHNSON

Jennifer Johnson keeps out of the rain
And sits on the toilet counting her change.
Sister of Mercy, flowers in her hair,
Stooped clerks and shoppers stop, stand and stare
At the old woman with beer can in hand
With nowhere to go but who shuffles and
Whispers from Pierhead to South Docks and down
By the Dingle and then back towards town,
Passed the Cathedral off Parliament Street,
Paint-peeling ceilings and dirty concrete,
Dust-covered windows and damp rotting rooms,
Girls on street corners, cheap smelling perfume,
Spiked railings and schoolboys who whistle and jeer
At Jennifer Johnson drinking her beer,
Catching the drips from her chin as she swears,
Cursing the schoolboys for nobody cares
For the old woman in ill-fitting clothes.
But where does she come from? Nobody knows.

GORE BROOK

"D'yer know," the young boy said,
throwing bread on the clear water
where the river stood still,
"why they call this the river that bled?"
The old man, wheel-chair bound
in his straight-jacket years,
watched the child turnaround,
and the ducks on the calm
waters beside the weir
where life's reflections disappear.
"No, do you?" the old man lied.
"This is where warriors were killed,"
the ten-year old replied,
proud of the battles that once raged
on the river bank where he played.
"More than a hundred died,"
the excited child cried.
The old man smiled and nodded;
he knew the gore that once flowed
was from the tanyard on the brow
with its black stench and wane,
and that gave Gore Brook its name.
Seventy years ago, another boy
had squeezed the tannin sap
from the oak and chestnut bark
for the dye pits above the park.
But the new boy would never know

the smell of death that filled the leat.
"Am off now," the boy shouted.
walking towards the terraced street.
Alone on the small green plot
by the river he once made red,
the old man heard echoes on the hill:
"More than a hundred died,"
The young boy cried.
But the Gore Brook was transient:
it left no epitaph or mark
of the old man in the park.

AMORÉ

This green oasis they call a municipal park
(but with exclusions like 'NO ADMISSION AFTER DARK')
was built to remind the industrial working-class
that the world was not all concrete grey, but trees and grass,

where creaking swings and roundabout on sharp
gravel base taught children how to handle the sight
of blood with grace and comprehend biology at advanced level,
or assess opposing concepts like God and devil.

But the church and council deemed the park a place where lust
and fornication could flourish freely after dusk;
so before the war they built railings around the park
and locked the gates every night, ten minutes before dark.

In 1940, the bars were removed, it was said
to make ammunition from the iron and the lead,
and, unregulated, the park stayed open all night
for lovers to copulate in comfort, out of sight.

But by then the local men had gone away to war,
and up the hill, close to the park, huts were built to store
those Italian prisoners of war who'd arrived
via land and sea, sentenced to spend their time inside.

By 1945 they had made themselves at home
and, with misguided authority, allowed to roam
with the few housewives who were more than willing to please,
while their soldier-husbands were clearing up overseas.

Now sex was a subject taboo until twelve in class,
but outside of school before our time and in the grass,
or concealed like commandos by foliage and leaves,
we studied nature with a bird's eye view from trees.

And then a couple hurried across the sloping field
to the dark corner of the park where (they thought) concealed
from prying eyes, they'd communicate by touch and sound.
We held our breath lying on branches above the ground

and watched them walk towards us, seemingly unattached –
but in a line she followed him to the flat grass patch
where she placed her red Sunday coat, lining to the ground.
Tenderly, her POW friend lowered her down.

"*Amoré*," he whispered to Mrs Brown. "*Amoré*."
The same word he'd used the day before with Mrs Grey.
"*Oh, go on, Luigi, not just yet. You are a pest!*
"*Amoré*," he said, his hand between her blouse and vest.

"*Luigi! You Italians are fast. Don't rush me;*
you'll be giving me 'iccups. I've not long since 'ad tea."
"*Amoré*," he repeated, with a hand on her knee.
"*Amoré! Don't you know any English, Luigi?*"

Like students encircling the operating table,
it was mobile anatomy that we were able
to analyze, and, with bated breath and racing heart,
we watched as silent shadows crept across the park.

Mr Bert Brown was still abroad and wearing khaki,
but Mrs Brown's thoughts were on the colour green, the tree
to be precise, where she'd seen a movement in the leaves.
It took her a minute to recognize Eric Jeeves.

Eric, my pal, lived across the street from Mrs Brown,
and, knowing he'd been spotted, decided to slide down
the tree and, without looking back, fled across the green
while Mrs Brown pulled down her skirt and began to scream.

Improperly dressed in his POW grey suit,
Luigi sprang to his feet and took-off in pursuit,
and shouted: "*You leetle swine. I'll sleet your throat.*"
Confused, Mrs Brown buried her head beneath her coat.

With padded shoulders and skirts that climbed above the knee,
throughout that summer the ladies continued to see
their Latin lovers, Luigi and Antonio,
but now having to take turns with their neighbours, Lil and Flo.

Having left their seeds with Mrs Brown and Mrs Grey,
at the summer's end, the POWs went away.
That year we had heard much talk of love (or amoré),
but could only guess what Bert and Stan would have to say.

THE STRANGER

Visiting his childhood days,
the old man heard a voice call
from the municipal park
where the shallow stream sat still.
'Hey there, come on down,' it called
through trees that now lined the hill.
But he walked along the brow,
watching the children and grass
and his past move in the breeze;
while the park birds sang unseen.
'Hurry up,' whispered the leaves
on trees where no trees had been.
For a moment, he lingered
by the field where he once played;
but mothers, a third his age,
watched the old man with the cane.
'On yer way.' one of them raged
at the man on memory lane.
From his past, he walked away,
and the child inside the man
for the first time saw decay.

THE MONASTERY

Bound by Victorian
leg-irons of ancient
and scarred desks where others
too had trembled before
a young woman in black,
now gaunt and bent of back.
"Quiet," she shrieked. Wide-eyed
and assertive, she slammed
her willow rod against
the partly opened door.
"Don't let me hear you breathe,"
she snarled, stamping the floor
to stir the dust and tears.
After a breathless pause,
the old nun laid the cane
across the table top
and, with interlocked hands,
continued: "Now we pray."
And the forty children
with elbows on their desks
began: "…give us this day".
"Close your eyes, you bad boy,"
the taut teacher shouted,
bending a creaking knee
before the five-year old,
terrified and weeping.
Outside, in soft sandals,

friars shuffled sockless
past the room with the rod
where perhaps they too had
first felt the wrath of God.

But I cast off the chains
that had anchored my roots
to industrial grime
and navy boiler-suits.

The seasons came and went
and in those missing years
two generations died
of cigarettes and beers.

Once a community
of Anglo-Saxon pride,
now only one old aunt
held back the Asian tide.

In her OAP flat,
we talked of years gone by,
of bowler hats and Whit-Walks
and home-made apple-pie.

"I'll see you in two weeks,"
I said outside her door
where the communal odours
matched the brown walls and floor.

On my way out of town
I drove towards my past

where, like the empty streets,
the sky was overcast.

In 89, the nuns
and friars moved away,
but the church looked unchanged
in shades of red and grey.

It didn't looked decayed
as I'd heard the news tell,
but I walked through the door
into an empty shell

where sparrows flew freely,
or wallowed in the mud,
and broken bricks and stone
lay where the pews once stood.

Like the stained-glass windows,
the pieta had gone
with the lead and fittings
and clergy's demijohn.

Within these walls at Mass
the crowd arrived roughshod,
stout-hearted in liquor
to show their faith in God.

Where in early April
excited bride and groom
queued and were sanctified
with a Catholic womb.

I thought I was alone
until a tapping came
from behind a slab stone
where a youth carved his name.

"What are you doing?" I said,
seeing vandalism at work -
and inside a church at that!
He blew away the dirt.

"*What's it ter yer?*" he replied.
"*This was a place for prayer,*"
I fumed, but felt foolish
defending disrepair.

"*This is a monastery,*"
I yelled. "*A place of God.*"
The skinhead turned and said:
"*I couldn't give a sod.*"

"*Doesn't your school teach you
about the Holy Ghost,
Matthew, Mark, Luke and John,
the Virgin Mary, son?*"

"*I don't know nowt about
ghosts and that Matthew gang;
and the virgins I know
are third or second 'and.*"

Staring into my eyes,
he bared his yellow teeth

while his blade continued
to probe the altar piece.

"Christ," he cried, and I thought
he'd seen the Saviour –
but it was his own blood
drawn by misbehaviour.

"You stupid old bugger,
look what you've made me do."
He seethed with phlegm and rage:
"This is because of you."

He mixed his young red blood
with the monastic dust
then turned to face the wall
and stabbed and bled and cussed.

Was it retribution
sent down from up above?
The nun said He sees all
combining fear with love.

Infinity? OK!
But two eyes seeing all?
Well that was a theory
that made no sense at all.

Perhaps there is a God,
a kind of local cop,
but who they overlooked
the day they shut up shop?

"Would you like a tissue
to wipe the blood away?"
"Listen, mate," he snapped back,
"be careful what you say."

"Are you a Catholic?"
I asked the irate youth
that nature and nurture
had trained to be uncouth.

He ignored the question
and filled his name with gore.
"This was my school," I said,
"*where caning was the law*."

"They caned yer? With a stick?
You should 'ave sent 'em down
for bleedin' GBH,"
the youth said, with a frown.

"They used the cane and strap
without fail everyday."
Now the youth was listening
to what I had to say.

"I wouldn't stand for that."
the youth said with a smirk.
"If they tried it on me
I'd butt the stupid berk."

*"I think it did us good.
It taught us wrong from right,
and we rubbed on the resin
to take away the bite.*

*"We also had prayers, three
or four times every day.
In here or at the desk
we'd close our eyes and pray.*

Do you support the church?"
I asked the shabby youth.
*"Naw, I'm like me old man,
a Man United fan."*

Like a boy I once knew,
he looked familiar,
even his ragged clothes
seemed strangely similar:

half the woollen goal posts,
and scuffed brown shoes worn thin
from kicking cobblestones
and tearing naked skin.

When the youth departed,
I heard the black priesthood
chanting in the Latin
that no-one understood.

A place of deep shadows,
confessionals at night,

but when the roof collapsed
the worshippers saw the light.

I left the church behind,
content that I'd survived,
and passed through spaces where
the Sanctus-bell had thrived:

streets that once housed people
who coughed the same stale air,
cowed beneath the long rod,
and lived on hope and prayer.

ROUTINE

With the odours of another day,
stepped out of bed; roof-tops and decay.
Two cold feet and oilcloth on the floor,
another week knocking Monday's door.

In an old flat cap and gabardine
coat, stood in line for number thirteen,
then moved upstairs with silent tongues,
cigarette smoke and fermenting lungs.

With holes in the soles of shoes and socks,
fell in line at the clocking-in box,
and with a whistle from foreman Sam,
like a metronome, his day began:

twelve hours at a rotating machine,
thirty minutes in the works' canteen;
a breathless bus in the creeping rain,
obscenities on the window pane.

A weary key in the latch at eight,
cockroaches and cinders in the grate,
egg and aspirin with two rounds of bread,
then counting bolts in a restless bed.

AD CAPTANDUM VULGUS

Between the mill and ancient spires,
the crippled knocker-up conspires
to raise the workers from their beds
with a ten foot pole and wire threads.
They traipse to work in discontent
at gothic mills where cog-wheels grind
their flesh and mind with overtime
that every weekend pays the rent.
On Friday night, in self-defence,
they pay God's agent Peter's Pence,
and then absolved, they stand in line
beneath the fish and chip shop sign
for supper wrapped in left-wing news
that formulate collective views.

THE ENTERTAINER

Alone, like a lost child grown old
on nicotine and acid rain,
the grey man stood on the corner,
a street-dancer without a name.

Humble at the factory gate
where the black walls were ten feet tall
to seal-in the machines and men
until the midday's siren call.

In overalls and on the move,
the oily crowd poured on the street,
as the old man with upturned cap
played a tune with his dancing feet.

Like a puppet in wooden shoes,
a wrinkled face and rheumy eyes,
for the half-pennies on the ground
he stamped his clogs in double time.

In hollow cheeks he sucked his gums,
and tap, tap, tapped a tune on stone;
a shuttle on a concrete loom,
every Friday afternoon.

END OF AN ERA

From its eyrie, the one-eyed clock,
as Gothic as a guillotine,
glared own on the rookery town
of boiler suits and nicotine.

"Don't be late," the timekeeper cried,
"Or we'll dock you half a day."
At six o'clock they punched their cards
and production was under way.

At cotton mills and down the mine,
with molten lead to galvanize,
the welder, turner and millwright
with engineers worked through the night.

In tallow-grease and paraffin,
with screw drivers, saws and hammers,
and blood-stained hands they rasped and grasped and
manipulated spanners.

On the turgid factory floor
the flywheels spun their pirouettes
and lubricated hearts and minds
with noxious fumes and cigarettes.

For a hundred and fifty years,
they broke their back but took the blame,
and then one day the unions came
with promises of wealth and fame.

But the Eastern sun was rising
and ploughs and rakes were cast away
as the trading tide was turning;
it seems the West had had its day.

With the ring of the final bell,
the factory gates were opened wide
and the workers, battered and bruised,
were carried on the ebbing tide

to street corners with leisure time,
decreasing jobs but increasing crime,
with opiates to ease the pain
and illustrate the wax and wane.

The circus came to town one day.
It stayed a while then went away.

ONCE UPON A TIME

Once upon a time, a factory
at the top of our terraced street
made elaborate chamber-pots
with roses and forget-me-nots
screen-printed for the antique trade,
all proudly labelled: 'British Made'.

Behind the gas works and Co-op,
real multicoloured trains were built
with sweat and blood and ferrous steels
and massive calibrated wheels
that travelled the world and conveyed
their brass-plaqued message: 'British made'.

Up the road from the loco sheds,
like a black lobster on the hill,
William Arkwright's four-story mill
shuttled shuttles throughout the night
weaving cloth for dye work tanks
with the appendage: 'Made in Lancs'.

The weekend work and double time
brought Rock'n'Roll in fifty-nine
and tattooed arms and bitter beer
and little extras for the wife
like stilettos and fishnet tights.
They thought they all had jobs for life.

The Loco was the first to close,
it locked its gates in sixty-nine,

and, when Arkwright turned off the heat,
the bulldozers rolled down our street
and uprooted the railway line
with its 'Made in Great Britain' sign.

Between green hills and Burger King
where once a thousand workers toiled
to keep the export market oiled,
a cash-and-carry super store
sells plastic goods in paper bags
attached to 'Made in China' tags.

GLYN CEIRIOG

In polished shoes and Sunday best
And regimental rows,
He in a hat and thermal vest,
She with her hair in bows.

He's six feet down below the ground,
She's four feet and a jot,
With feet to east they're westward bound,
Carnations in the pot.

Buried in lipstick and cologne
And rouge and wedding ring,
But his shaved chin now turned to bone
And Windsor knot to string.

Her tongue now still as four a.m.,
She wore his ears to stone.
She was the pain of valley men,
Her verbal skills home-grown.

The birds have flown, they left their sign,
The vultures came and fed,
Now Ethel's on his rosehip wine
With Cyril in their bed.

For economy in twos or more
This dogless land of nod;
No headstones for those right of door!
How will they talk with God?

Here amid dust and bones
And good Welsh names like Glyn and Jones,
Alone with tales to tell,
Is 19th century Jane Morrell.

As silent as the church step fly,
They lie beneath the grass
Until they greet the next to die
And that will surely pass.

So remember these words I speak
And go to St. Ffradds every week,
Then, in Glyn Ceiriog when you're ill,
You're more than welcome on the hill.

HIGH TIDE

It was a stormy New Year's Eve on the
slippery half-mile long, four persons wide,
semi-circular, coast-to-coast divide,
awash with an eleven metre tide.

Those promenading, hoop-skirted ladies
a hundred years before would not foresee
that one day a solitary soul would be
walking biblically across the sea.

Like small waves, a hundred common gulls sprawled
on the lee side of the seaweeded wall,
while on the open sea, black-backed gulls trawled
and foraged fearlessly beneath the squall.

'Beware of the offshore wind and wave-form,'
the dock notice read – but he thought the storm
would pass and the strip of blue would transform
the twin dangers of which the notice warned.

In the beginning, he walked through the seaweed
but with confidence that he could proceed,
despite the gale-force wind and churning sea
that was now bombarding this man-made quay.

At the halfway mark, the sea was severe,
but the crashing, waist high waves at his rear
were whipped by a depression to confirm
that he had reached a point of no return.

Moving slowly, with his life in peril,
he listened to the oystercatchers' shrill
calls as they pushed and jostled for the thrill,
so like the screams that made his world stand still

when the storm broke and day turned into night.
He slipped but initially kept upright,
cursing his own stupid lack of foresight
and the wet, thirty degree Fahrenheit.

Where the land conjoins the harbour wall, he
stumbled, crawling like a beached manatee,
but dragged himself clear of the raging sea
as it finally overwhelmed the quay.

He was reminded as he stood drying
that storms are overcome not by crying;
and that he would not have been soaked in brine
had he taken note of the warning sign.

AFTER THE TIDE

Beside a shallow channel left
by the ebbing tide, a figure,
bent double and in silhouette,
dug a trench in search of lugs and
built a wall ten feet long of sand.

A shelduck, sharp in black and white,
ratcheted up from the sea stream,
slow and low away from the man,
its red-beaked mate followed quietly,
flying to a nearby island.

At the cross-roads of sea and land,
curlews waded in search of food,
and between the veiled sea and man
a thousand burrowing knots dug
for prey – but built no wall of sand.

HOUSE TO RENT

It was the council that cleared
the smell of death and decay
from the dark corner cupboard
where the child had left its dust
sixty years ago at play.
And brown-flowered paper peeled
from the walls like eight-ply rust.

Built in 1864
of black brick and Welsh grey slate
with flagged floor and iron grate
(to house the industrial poor),
the soot-stained two-up-and-down
stood free of humanity
as it had four times before.

But there once lived a new bride,
firm of breast, buttock and wrist
who would donkey-stone the step
and at sink and bed perspire
to fulfil her wifely roles.
In time she became a sage
and her neighbours bared their souls.

When her husband died, the house
fell into damp disrepair
with old fermenting odours.
And, like the shadows in the night,
she began to transmutate
to that stranger on the street…
Then they came to fumigate.

LITTLE GIRLS

"I'm a model for Vogue," one cried,
and twisted and brushed back her locks
for the man with the little black box,
while another pushed her aside.

"'er a model?" a third replied,
"She's nowt but the Gretham Street lag,
but to friends she's Beryl the bag!"
In friendship they jostled and vied.

"Of course it's me they wanna see."
the first one smiled, tilting her head.
"No, it's me," the second girl said,
while the quiet one asked: *"What's the fee?"*

SUNDAY MORNING

At midnight
with firm resolve intact,
she turned her head, refused
to commit the act.

But macho
was equal to the task
and by deceit infused
behind a mannered mask.

She lay down
with voices in her head
that argued with the church
and stranger on her bed.

And when dawn
had chased her swain away,
the contradictions lurched
unwanted into day.

Now someplace
between heaven and hell,
she sits alone, disgraced
by Sunday's solemn bell.

VOICES IN THE DARK

Late evening, alone with a bottle or
two, CNN, Palestine, unjust war
raging between Jew, Sunni and Shiite;
recession: a typical winter's night.
The constant rain against the windowpane,
rat-a-tat-tatting like Columbine High
where ordinary kids screamed die, die, die.
But rat-a-tat-tat was the rain's refrain
as it tapped repeatedly on my window pane.
I closed the curtains to silence the storm
that rattled the windows and stirred the air,
while the fire's reflection danced on the wall;
and I fell asleep in my rocking chair.
Mutilated bodies, a piercing scream,
I struggled to wake from the dreadful dream
where children were boiled in molten lead,
but some invisible force held me down
while a face talked about a buried town,
and quantified the day's injured and dead.
I wanted to run but couldn't escape
from the informer with the floating face
that talked fluidly of torture and rape.
Describing how the destruction began,
it revealed those places on earth like hell,
and soon I was falling under the spell
of the floating face with a tale to tell.
It spoke of criminal devastation,

and terrible acts of God - not Satan:
thousands of dead was the estimation,
said the intruder in conversation;
an unwanted messenger of death and vice
who was so knowledgeable and precise.
But then it began to guess and debate
about abstractions at some future date.
However, as if to extrapolate
for those of sensitive disposition,
the speaker announced a pre-condition:
"Viewers should be warned that the following
contains scenes that may be deemed harrowing,
and considered by some as a war crime,"
(Opinion will be divided by race).
"*Of course many civilians have been killed,*
but that's unavoidable in wartime,"
a spokeswomen, with cropped hair and skilled
at inverting cause and effect, intervened,
and opined that intervention would fail
as nature decrees the strong shall prevail.
Annoyed by her affinity with hate,
and obvious disregard for the dead,
my next concern, I'm sorry to relate,
was whether to pour myself white or red.

ALONE

Ragged from grey head to flip-flop
feet, and littering yesterday's bread,
the old woman with a Co-op
bag seems not afraid to contravene
the keep-off notice on the green.

And we sit together, alone,

where city pigeons congregate,
silk-smooth, alert, and vacillate
near the feet of the drunken man
who shares the feral bread and sups
Carlsberg Special brew from its can.

And we watch together, alone,

as vehicles and crowds transmutate
around the down-town green estate,
tic-tocking like the town hall clock.
where haves and have-nots re-unite
until the still electric night.

And we walk together, alone.

At dusk, an old tramp rests his head
on the hardwood bench, his bed,
beneath memorials of wars
and liquid crystals on the stores;
and, like the tramp, we sleep alone.

GERIATRIC

She sits on the edge of the chair
In a cold ward of eight lost souls
Now geriatric grey and bent,
A woollen blanket heaven sent.

But beneath the arthritic pain
In features from antiquity
There's an elegance that remains
With gestures of femininity.

Like a flower sucked dry of life,
Its seeds well scattered on the wind,
Alone she stares back into time
At untold stories in her mind.

But the woman refined of face
In winceyette and fluffy shoes
Prays every night to die –
For her, it's living that's the lie.

DOWNTOWN

One o'clock on Friday and all seems well:
dark suits, smoke, cheese-on-toast, another
day; repetitions of fifty years before
with Ada, white and deaf, behind the bar

breathing the disinfected city dust.
"*Two pints of mild, love.*' Cig-ends on the floor.
The old barmaid cups an ear, creaks and leaks
veiled perspiration as she steers the years.

Shoulder to shoulder in self-interest,
clerks and travellers in percentages talk,
but middle-aged vulnerability
watches itself in the cracked white tiled wall.

Through the window the winter sun deceives.

CONDITIONING

For an hour on the doorstep she waited
for the very first boy she had dated;
but, the subject of mirth and down-hearted,
she crept back down the street and departed.

AWAKENING

Last night we laughed, outside was dark;
it kept us warm. Now comes the dawn.

BACK TO FRONT

The kindest thing to all mankind:
the front's the front and back's behind.

THE DISCO

The smell of sweat and the cheap perfume,
the emptiness of the crowded room.

GRIEF

'You do! He once lived on our street.
I see him at the cemetery,'
she said, trying to be discreet.

But I couldn't recall the man
bent over in a cloud of smoke
gently building a house of sticks.

Intense and alone, and playing
with the ring on his third finger,
he studied the wooden structure.

At ten, and making for the door,
we passed him, a whisky in hand,
the scattered matchsticks on the floor.

"That's right! They moved a year ago,
and six months later she was dead" .

CITY NIGHTS

An eye, peep-holing from within
the city centre gaming den.
A creaking door, invited in.
Ring-fingered women and their men,
round shouldered and optimistic
at a table sliding plastic.
But the Gordon's gin and tonic
and rotating wheel proves toxic.
Not to worry, they've more of that
for loaded dice and baccarat.

The papers at the Daily News
fall off the press with printed views
while process workers congregate
outside the door and delegate
a Scouser, guttural and irate,
to be their leader designate.
And on the lamp-lit street they shout:
'increase our pay or we'll all walk out,'
but then demand a paradigm
of a shorter week with overtime.

On the corner of Oxford Street,
remnants of the day's football meet,
green and blue and diametric,
fist to fist and isometric,
But lacerations undermine
tribal colours and redefine
the green and blue to crimson red,

uniting opponents in bloodshed.
In black and white but trimmed with steel,
it's law v juvenile kriegspiel.

In an A & E anteroom,
a doctor scrapes a six inch wound
while a scanner searches in vain
for a football fan's alleged brain.
But on a gloss-black plastic bed
(for the incontinent or dead?)
a protagonist seems content
to sleep it off from now till Lent.
At the Infirmary's A & E
this service, vis-à-vis, is free.

HI HO, HI HO

The dying night bequeathed the dawn
a thin grey mist that weatherworn
and ragged rolled across the sea
to where black waters lapped the quay.

And there, aching at bow and stern,
a ferryboat groaned on the swell,
its rattling chains against the rail,
as mournful as St. Nick's church bell.

A shoreman unwound the bollard,
throwing the hawser at the boots
of the deckhand with frozen hands;
an undulating journeyman.

Sea-salt and diesel spiced the air,
and, like old bones before first light,
a gangway creaked and fell to earth
while seagulls screeched and fought in flight.

Like shadows on a wooden hill,
the solemn commuters waited,
but the man in the black peak cap
watched the clock and aggravated

the motley mass en-route to work.
As rigid as the ferry's beams,
at eight o'clock they walked the plank,
dragging onboard their fading dreams.

In borrowed space, they sat in rows
where crinolines and spats once passed,
for, like those long-dead folk, they are
the regulated working class.

Side-by-side, and inside their heads,
the Wirral girls in fur-lined boots
and clerks in white and red, or blue,
sat thinking of their still warm beds.

Oilskin wrapped on an outer deck
and turtle-necked against the rain,
the nomad of rope and anchor
struggled to lift the gangway chain.

With grating power, the turgid
waters lurched metamorphic white,
and the urban crew sailed towards
the two stone monuments in flight.

At the Liverpool landing stage,
the human tide, like black beetles
exposed to light, scurried away,
conformists for another day.

THE HAND

It was the eve of another birthday
and I watched the soft hand moving the pen
as it searched for a word to rhyme with time
the way a blind man walks behind his stick.
There were more brown spots than I could recall
when they marked my growing pains on the wall.

My father was not a scholarly man -
his labours were on the factory floor -
but his brush strokes could make swans skate on snow
and crippled beggars waltz the Barcarolle.
Fine art compared to my acerbic rod
that computes percentages and cash flow.

But no captured words or imagery
could recreate my black and white picture
of him standing suited against the sun.
Like a businessman with bandaged hand,
in cycle-clips and triangular sling:
a day off work for losing half-a-thumb.

The years of wrestling with quarter-inch thick
wire in Galvani's molten bath that writhed
like steaming snakes could not intimidate
the shapes he sculpted from sulphurous lead,
while the slimmer hand of his eldest son
fought nothing more than the commercial pen.

He was a man proud of his old flat cap,
ragged overalls, barbed wounds and broken bones.
No self-praise or fancy intonations
from the artisan with gravel hands
that held mine when I sat on his shoulders
and led me to the cherry blossom lands.

I listened to the wood pigeons cooing
and lawn-mower men while wigged women in
cultured teeth stare through Venetian blinds
at their neighbours in four-bedroom detached.
A town where middle-aged and middle-classed
wear their designer labels on their hats.

There were only two stanzas to write but
it was growing dark and I fell asleep
to dream of inefficient lawyers,
accountants' fees and Value Added Tax,
of high bank charges and low sales returns,
the minimum wage on the camel's back.

When I awoke on my sixty-second,
I saw my father in the looking-glass,
and the black priest and burial balm;
but the tired face faded behind the steam.
He had appeared older than yesterday -
as did the softer hands he had bequeathed.

THE BACK-ALLEY SINGER

Perhaps it was the harmony between
the abstract elements of sky and sound
that activated a long-forgotten scene,
veiled but indelible and profound.

Or could the trigger have been physical
like the pretty girl, bashful yet serene?
Or the irksome and annoying signal
of a barking dog, distant and unseen?

August 1945, and no war;
but Sunday midday, in that regard,
was unchanged: potatoes, mince and coleslaw,
a dog barking in a back-to-back yard.

"What a lovely song, but so very sad.
I think it's Vera Lynn," Mam said to Dad.
"Turn up the sound."
                "I'd 'ave a job," Dad replied.
"Because whoever's singing is outside."

First it was a murmur then a whisper
growing sweeter as it slowly filled
the room; then the words became much crisper,
like a daffodil bursting into bloom.

Standing by the backdoor, Dad said to Mam:
"It's a woman with two kids and a pram".
Mother, in her Sunday-best pinafore,
went to see what the woman was singing for.

"Said 'er 'usband didn't come back from the war,
and she's three children. I gave 'er a sweet
coupon and one-and-six pence," Mam explained.
"I told 'er she'd make more singing on street,
but the young lass said she was too ashamed."

TWENTY LINES ON A LIFE

Sunlight slanted across the living room.
It was mid-morning and my mother stood
cradling my baby sister to her chest.
Knee-high, I held on to her flowered dress.
"Hello, love," the woman from next door said,
walking into the house, red faced and round
and sucking her gums as though chewing bread.
"How long, love?" she asked, with a rasping sound.
She touched the infant's head and a tear fell
from my mother's cheek on the swaddling clothes;
and the women, two generations apart,
faced each other in the warm morning sun
while my sister I were in the dark.
"She looks lovely, love. It's hard to believe
she's dying. Are you sure that's what he said?"
My mother nodded. "Don't cry, Mam," I begged,
and Pauline moved her head, looking at me.
"Oh, God, she's dead" the old woman exclaimed.
"No, she's looking at her brother." Mam sighed.
But then the baby's head fell to the side.

DANCING WITH FRED ASTAIRE

Blonde and willow slim, an inviting smile,
she was belle of the ball in '46,
with Evening in Paris behind her ear,
a cigarette holder and painted lips.

In their Palais-de-Dancing patent shoes,
the Romeos in starched striped collars queued,
and over-excused the 'excuse-me' dance
while her sequins shimmered to drum and sax.

She listened to the whispered mating calls
from the brilliantine-smooth men of war
but she'd left her thoughts in the front seats stalls,
and vowed love for all but loved none at all.

Living with mam and dad in '59,
she did piece-work and overtime and watched
the Black and White Minstrels on the tele,
and on Sunday went to church with Nellie.

In the late sixties, the factory closed
and the corner shops were falling down.
Unemployed and family in decline,
a brown couple moved into number nine.

In the summer '77,
with posters and saris she'd never seen,
Bombay and Karachi moved into town
and, like her love letters, the street turned brown.

In '88 and feeling out of place,
with greying hair, thin lips and ashen face,
her new neighbours talked with inflections rare,
and her only white neighbour said 'don't stare'.

In '99, in an old person's flat,
on the first floor with pillows for support,
she sat alone and sprayed for daily breath,
and muttered to herself of this and that.

But now and again on Radio Two,
she'd hear the strings of Rhapsody in Blue,
and in a satin dress and flowered hair,
she was dancing again with Fred Astaire.

PRIVATE CONVERSATIONS

"My novel is not about family,"
I told my late-mother's sister, Cathy
who lives alone in a flat-type attic
surrounded by crime, and xenophobic.

"It starts in 1926," I said,
"and most of the characters are now dead."
"I was only a girl then." she replied.
"That's when we first went to the seaside.

"Yer mam and me and yer granddad and gran
went to Blackpool and we 'ad chips and scran.
I can remember it like yesterday:
went by chara and the driver lost 'is way."

"Some names may sound familiar." I explained,
wondering how Cathy would view the maimed
ex-soldier called Will, from the First World War,
like her own dad, henpecked and battle-sore.

"Are you leaving this book for me to read?"
she asked, an inhaler helping her breathe
easier, having just said more than she'd
said all week. "Yes, it's for you, " I agreed.

"I can't read much more than a page a day.
It's not about sex that they seem to play

on the TV everyday, is it?
Meself, I prefer a good whodunnit."

I explained it was a tale of decay,
about those grey streets where she used to play,
and where she had lived for 83 years.
A tale of survival, laughter and tears.

"What decay is that?" she asked with a frown,
her thin neck stretching from her dressing gown
of faded flowers buttoned to the chin.
She seemed to have forgotten the vermin.

"Don't you recall the beetles in the hearth,
the flagged backyard with the coal and tin bath?
Kneeling in the cold with the Evening News
trying to light a fire? Holes in the shoes?"

It wasn't like that," she said with a smile
that suggested my recall was facile.
"We kept the tin bath on a nail in the shed,
and dad made the fire while I was in bed."

Somebody had to make the fire, I thought,
with bits of wood and paper for support.
And boil the water on the fireside hob,
then draw the blind for Saturday night's swab.

"Don't you remember those back-alley screams
that could have been outside or in your dreams?
The drunks falling about in the shadows;
the spluttering gaslight and the psychos?"

"I hope you haven't written that stuff down,"
she said, with serious concern for her town.
"We've got Sunny Brow and other nice parks –
and in our street we 'ad two town 'all clerks!

We 'ad real good neighbours when I was small,"
she said, with pride, but I seemed to recall
the walls were so thin, you heard neighbours fight,
and often in the middle of the night.

Of course, with deference to kin and age,
I consider it wise not to engage
in that debate, keeping thoughts in my head.
But, deciding to put my case, I said:

"It was boiled egg and chips for Thursday's tea,
and during the war they used to fill me
with bread and dripping, and that other treat:
through to Wednesday eating Sunday's cold meat."

"We 'ad other things," she said with a frown.
"You could feed a family for 'alf-a-crown.
There was pig's trotters and tripe and cow-'eel.
None in our family ever missed a meal.

"If you've said we went without, it's not true.
I'm sorry; I don't want to upset you,
but you'll give some people the wrong idea,
like thinking all the wages went on beer."

"A high percentage of income was spent
on cigarettes and beer and, or course, rent,"
I replied, determined to put my side
without any intention to misguide.

"Don't you remember, Cathy, how some lived?
As a kid I saw first-hand the squalid
homes; stuffing out of chairs, ash in the grate,
and how the council used to fumigate."

"That's news to me; never 'eard owt like that.
In all me life I've never seen a rat.
The roaches used to come in with the coal,
but yer granddad kept 'em under control."

Her memory's sound. Perhaps she didn't know
how, when the toxic gas began to flow
from the van to the house next-door-but-two,
we stood outside because the fumes passed through.

"It was nowt to do with me what went on.
When I got 'ome from work, the day was done.
I wore me treadlin' shoes six days a week,
and putting up me feet was Sunday's treat.

"In winter I didn't see a neighbour
for months on end. It was like 'ard labour
'avin' to make-up twelve dresses an hour
with me own feet switching on the power.

"It were toes down to go, 'eels down to stop,
all day long at that Manchester sweatshop.

Me poor legs felt like two lumps of lead,
and that's probably why I never wed.

"Me fingers were sore and me eyes bloodshot."
"Twelve dresses an hour seems an awful lot,"
I suggested, studying her bent back.
"We worked in threes and you soon got the knack.

"With two sewers, I did the overlock,
but all day long we worked against the clock.
Yer mam worked with me before you were born,
and we were on the tram at crack of dawn.

"After a quick breakfast of bread and jam,
we'd put on 'at and coat and get on tram.
Some went by bike, and there were buses too.
You'd get up to a 'undred in the queue.

"The men went upstairs in their boilersuits,
clattering up and down in 'obnail boots.
Upstairs you could cut the air with a knife;
when you think, it was an un'ealthy life.

"A lot of water's gone under the bridge
since yer dad brought yer granny a cabbage
when 'e'd call courtin' yer mam after work;
and in the backyard 'is 'orse'd go berserk."

"Why was that?" I asked, absorbing the past.
"It seemed to know when it 'ad done its last
street call on the round selling fruit and veg.
And yer dad changed its name to Dot from Reg."

"I don't suppose it was pleased about that,"
I said, recalling a schoolboy called Pat.
"And yer mam didn't want to share her name
with an old Evening News 'orse, 'alf lame.

"It didn't stop 'er marryin' at all.
She got wed in white. There she is on the wall."
It was the picture that hung on a hook
when I was young – since described in my book.

Like a tortoise coming out of its shell,
she stretched her neck and began to expel
into her gaping mouth medication
that would help further clarification.

She was flicking the pages and reading
a line here and there, I felt like pleading
for her to put the book on the knee-high
table with her medicines and porkpie.

"Co-op?" she said, glasses before her face.
"Is that the one on 'yde Road, the same place
where we went to that wedding years ago,
when yer dad was troubled with lumbago?

"'ere, it was upstairs there we 'ad a 'am
salad after we 'ad buried yer gran.
And we 'ad that great big room just to us,
and the undertaker made such a fuss."

On a cold and wet winter afternoon
sitting in the middle of a vast room
with paper tablecloth and serviette
was not an occasion I could forget.

The previous Saturday afternoon –
when granny had died in the living room –
Cathy, running around the house, went wild,
screaming and shouting like a distraught child.

Now, ten years past her mother's final age,
but imprisoned like a bird in a cage
by emphysema on an upper floor,
she lives alone with five locks on the door.

"That's much better," she said, patting her chest
and replacing the spray can with the rest
of her daily needs on the small table
by her side, "but still unemployable."

She smiled, and we looked behind each other's
eyes. Her skin was stretched tight like her mother's
face had been the year before she expired.
"How was the hospital trip?" I enquired.

"And what did they report about the test
they did on your waterworks and the rest
of your problems down below the waistline?"
I asked, and she replied: "They said it's fine."

Quite separate from her emphysema,
she said the woman doctor had seen her

about the blood she found in her urine
and told her to halve the daily aspirin.

"I had a funny turn on the table
and got so flustered I wasn't able
to take in what she said about me 'eart,
but I 'eard 'er say it would stop and start."

"Did she mean missing a beat?" I enquired.
"I'm not sure. I was so excited and tired,
an' lyin' 'alf naked in a strange room'
but she thought there was nowt wrong with me womb.

"The doctor said it was as good as new
as I've never 'ad sex. We didn't do
things like that before marriage years ago;
so there'll be no wear and tear down below.

"But I'm not right since they tried to break in."
Three months before, youths had attacked the thin
front door with their feet until the door frame
came away while they called her by her name.

It was the bolt screwed not to frame but wall
that kept the gang on the communal hall.
"You should have dialled three nines," I said again,
but she said that would trouble the policemen.

"The kids knocked the door and asked for sugar,
but I shouted and said, go on, bugger
off, and then they started battering the door.
I crawled under the bed and lay on the floor."

I reassured her that with the deadlock
set, it would be impossible to knock
the replacement frame away from the wall
(I'd also put a camera in the hall).

She said the violence was worldwide and not
just where she'd spent her life. "There's not a lot
you can do about it. They've got guns now.
I've 'eard they use them when they 'ave a row!"

What she had to say about guns was true,
but it was the poor parts where violence grew.
"They see it all on the tele," she said.
"And single mums bringing up kids, I've read.

"There's no discipline in the schools these days.
The government's all talk and 'olidays',
like them do-gooders who wouldn't live 'ere
for five minutes, never mind a full year.

"It'll get worse and then the police won't cope
with all the kids robbing and taking dope.
They've got a lot to answer for, them MPs,
allowin' in the so-called refugees."

Not only had she lost most of her peers,
their replacements wear silks from shins to ears,
or pyjama trousers out on the street
and add strange smelling spices to their meat.

"I wish I could turn back the clock, you know,
for a night with yer mam at bingo.
Then we'd call in the Midland for a stout.
There'd be plenty for us to talk about."

On page 315, they're back together
in the pub sheltering from the weather;
one in a coat, the other in a mac,
for a mid-afternoon milk stout and snack.

Reading the novel may cause her distress
as it wouldn't be hard to guess
the cameo roles the family play
against a landscape of industrial grey.

"Do you mind if I take the book away?
I'll bring it back when I come next Saturday."
I said the last sentence with finger's crossed –
but on Cathy, the words I said were lost.

 "I'll keep your book until I've finished it,"
she said, offering me a tea biscuit.
"I'll ignore all the sex and violence."
She had a look of quiet defiance.

I watched my old aunt sitting in her chair,
devalued like one of a broken pair –
but capable of talking with those dead
members of her own family, she said.

She was turning the pages in the book
and, although intelligent, had the look

of a woman much older than her years,
alone with memories and souvenirs.

But I knew she was once one of a pair
of flappers with black berets and blonde hair,
and I can still see them in forty-eight
when arm-in-arm they seemed to illustrate

that the war was over and winter done.
There was the excitement of things to come,
and, like the roadside blossom in mixed hues,
the sun brought out cotton frocks and white shoes.

A ten year old out of church with a crowd
en-route to milk bar looked up and was proud
to meet relatives getting off the tram.
"Look, it's our Bernard," Cathy said to Mam,

laughing as though they would live forever;
and, according to Cathy, together
one day, as children again, they will be.
But where, in afterlife, will that leave me?

Will those reflections in the pages on
her knee take her back to those days long gone?
Does she, I wonder, remember the time
when the child saw the sisters in their prime?

With head inclined and chin upon her chest,
she'd fallen in a trance. She must be stressed,
I thought, studying the novel that lay
open on her knees, an arm's length away.

I dismissed the crass thought, crossing the room
to the sideboard with its bills, brush and comb
and framed pictures of the living and dead,
including gran and granddad when they wed;

she standing in frilly blouse and drawn waist,
he sitting, with flying collar and chaste.
In the sideboard mirror I saw my face
and suddenly I'd taken granddad's place.

"You've upset me," Cathy said from behind.
She hadn't fallen asleep but inclined
her head to read the same page several times.
"We never committed them kind of crimes."

"Crimes? What crimes?" I asked in all innocence.
"Books last for years," she said, in annoyance.
"The machinists didn't steal cloth like you've
written. I'm sorry, but I disapprove.

"Why, you've even named the place where I worked."
I felt the antagonism would get worse.
And I could already sense the outrage
when she reaches the wedding reception page.

"Why don't you apply for a ground-floor place?"
I said, trying not to look her in the face.
"I'd never be able to sleep at night.
Don't worry about me: I'll be all right."

Cathy's response was emphatic and she
had conditioned herself not to foresee
beyond the next meal. "With a ground-floor flat
you could walk down to the shops for a chat."

"Even if I could get to the shops, they're
all boarded and, anyway, I don't care
for going out for a bit of mince meat
with those 'ooligans out there on the street."

"How's the breathing?" I asked, as she inhaled.
"I'm still doin' it," she said, and exhaled
her medication as she gasped for air,
muttering her usual 'save-me-God' prayer.

Like an old frayed photograph, she stood at
the dark window of her OAP flat
and waved, holding my novel in her hand.
An ageing lady in a foreign land.

A WEEK LATER

"I'm parked outside Longsight street market
and should be at your door in a minute,"
I said to Cathy, the phone at my head,
watching a black man eat a stick of bread.

Longsight was a district once white and poor.
It still seemed poor but the whites were fewer,
and while most of the buildings looked the same,
the flavour was now curry and chow mein.

"I'll be behind the door to let you in,"
she replied, but sounding like stone on tin.
Either she had inhaled her medicine
or was about to dish out discipline.

"Are you okay?" I asked, still at the lights
where the coloured skins outnumbered the whites
by a ratio of thirteen to two,
and the posters, like the talk, were Urdu.

"Yes," she replied, but with less emphasis.
The tone of her voice said something was amiss.
"I'll put the kettle on. Do you want tea,
or are you still drinking that black coffee?"

"Still on the antibiotics," I said,
as the traffic lights changed to green from red,
and a group in saris and pantaloons
hurried by with helium-filled balloons.

Cathy was dressed from head to toe in black,
confirming that I was in for some flak.
"I'll go to the lav now I've let you in,"
she said, turning like paint-chipped porcelain.

The novel was on the knee-high table
with bookmark in place, and I was able
to see what I thought was page one three nine.
So far in the book in such a short time?

When the cistern flushed, I put the book down,
and she returned to her chair with a frown.

"When I get me breath back, I'll get you a cup."
Her expression confirmed something was up.

"You've upset me again, writing all that."
Able to guess what was coming, I sat
on the opposite chair and asked what she meant.
"I'm very un'appy with that comment."

"Look, Cathy' I've told you, it's all fiction,"
I said, attempting to put conviction
in my denial of what she may say.
"It's imagination. Like a stage play."

"See what you've written on page one six five.
You can't say that's imagination. I've
never read anything so 'orrible
about your granma. It's deplorable."

"Cathy, please don't take it to heart," I sighed.
"That woman is not your mother," I lied.
She leaned forward with her body in space,
and an unusual look crossed her face.

"I thought you were only on page one three nine?"
"It's there, right under 1939,"
she shouted. I could see it was hopeless.
"In 'er forties, 'er mother was toothless…"

She held the open book close to her face
and said what I'd written was a disgrace.
*"…'er thin and colourless lips painted red,
with peach rouge on each cheek,"* aloud she read.

"...Short 'air-like creases lined 'er upper lip."
I knew I was in for an awkward trip.
"And this bit's about me dad, I presume:
'is war-injured leg stretched into the room'.

"That's me Mam and Dad, and don't deny it.
Not only that, and you'll 'ave to admit,
I'm Eve, one of the sisters who may be,
according to this, 'avin' a baby!

"What will the neighbours say? They'll think it's me,
I'd better go an make a cup of tea,
and take an aspirin to settle me 'eart.
What you've written 'as given me a start."

"Make mine a black coffee, please. With one spoon."
I said, as Cathy shuffled from the room,
bowed and scratching an exposed collarbone.
I sat back, grateful to be left alone.

And thankful I hadn't described the love scene
between Eve and Herbert after they'd been
to see Clarke Gable and Carol Lombard,
and their interaction in the old churchyard.

In the past, that would have filled a whole page,
but I don't want to contemplate the rage
that my old aunt Cathy would undergo
had her fictional image stooped so low.

Cathy once owned a two-up and two-down
on the north side of the same Gorton town,
but she was re-housed by a clerk's decree
and allocated a council flat key.

Now you may think that a working-class town
is one shade of grey, but that is unsound
philosophy as any back-street kid
will say: the shades range from sour to putrid.

From the soot-black Victorian terraced
houses with their small dark rooms and fibrous
cobwebs, paint-splashed between wall and ceiling,
with six decades of flowered paper peeling,

and their peculiar smells of methane;
to those rows less tarnished by acid rain,
and with two extra cubic feet of air –
but still back-to-back and in disrepair.

And then there's the red-bricked, semi-detached
council houses with their walled-off and thatched
front gardens growing the odd broken chair,
and neighbours with their 'don't-look-at-me' stare.

"Are you sure you don't want some milk in it?"
she asked, spilling coffee on the carpet
from the chipped cup rattling on the saucer.
"It looks just like a cup of black water."

"United played badly today," I said.
"I think they're overpaid and overfed.

One's on ninety thousand a week," she cried,
placing the beverage on the tiled fireside.

"That's more than I earned in forty-nine years.
There's no justice in this world. It brings tears
to my eyes," she continued. "And they claim
it's talent, but it's only a kids' game."

Thankfully, her mind was off the novel,
and she began to rant how immoral
for someone to make in one week what she
earned from fourteen to sixty-three.

"And another thing." she said, changing tack.
"When we went shopping, yer mam wore a mac,
and I wore the coat. Of course, you knew that.
But 'ow did you know about the lilac

flowers yer mam carried when she got wed?"
Looking at the picture above her head
of the young woman with lilacs and lace,
I put an innocent look on my face.

"What flowers and coats are you talking about?"
"I'm not daft: I can see family throughout
yer book. You've even put the groom in grey,
and described the street and back alleyway.

"By the way, I've never seen a man crawl
down the street like that man who seems to fall
in yer book every time 'e's 'ad a drink.
That's in your imagination, I think."

"It's fact! There was a man who, without fail,
would crawl home after a night on the ale.
Yet when he went to work he looked quite smart
in the standard uniform of a clerk.

'Different alcohols affect the brain
in ways that vary between hop and grain,
or, in the case of legs, that decider
whether one walks or falls: scrumpy cider."

"Scrumpy cider? Whether it's true of not
I think you've made that bit up, like a lot
of what you've written. And I say your view
of your granma, me Mam, is just not true."

"I'm not going all over that again."
"No, because you're embarrassed, and when
you write about the ex-prisoner of war
as being called Will, you've said it all."

"When you read on, you'll see it's not your dad.
The man in the book called Will has a bad
chest, caused by too much smoking, but the cough
turns to emphysema and sees him off."

Cathy rearranged herself in the chair
and looked in my eyes with that wide-eyed stare.
Without thinking, I'd raised her condition,
caused not by fags, but toxic emission.

"When I was young, they called it bronchitis.
Everybody seemed to have an itis.
There was appendicitis, arthritis,
laryngitis and that dermatitis

"that you'd see on the backs of people's 'ands.
And the laryngitis affected the glands
up 'ere in the throat. Could 'ave been the smoke:
everybody was burning coal or coke.

"We were living on top of each other.
It's a wonder we didn't all smother
in those pea-soupers that used to come down,
and were so thick you couldn't see the ground.

"D'yer remember them fogs? They were yellow
and so thick and foul you couldn't swallow.
And when you put an 'anky to yer face,
it turned black like the back of the fireplace."

"Yes, I recall getting lost in the fog –
or smog – and feeling sick as a dog.
Hearing the fog signals and next door croaking
from carbon monoxide and chain-smoking."

"In the winter, all the people 'ad bad chests.
That's why we'd wear 'ats and woollen vests,
and I'd wrap a thick scarf around me 'ead;
but a lot of neighbours finished up dead.

"If the cause of death was on the 'eadstones,
it'd tell a story of 'ow them bones

went to the cemetery before their due,
because of so-called bronchitis and flu.

"When I was a girl, the men wore black suits
and flat caps on Sunday with lace-up boots,
and I'd see 'em walkin' to the public
'ouse like smokin' chimneys with asthmatic

"chests, and their backs bent as they coughed up
phlegm.
It was the smoke that put many of them
in an early grave, but they didn't know
that they would die from smokin' tobacco."

"And it was more addictive in those days,"
I said. "And the smoke poured from the railways,
factory boilers and domestic grates,
consuming coal by the hundredweights."

"Do you remember 'ow 'e delivered coal?
On 'is back, down the 'all to the coal-'ole.
Every time the coalman went down the 'all
yer gran put as little tick on the wall."

"Why was that?" I asked, unable to recall
any ticks on the brown lincrusta wall.
"To count the number of bags emptied. I've
'eard they would drop four and say it was five!"

"Cheating? In days when doors were left open?
"They weren't neighbours, you know. They were
tradesman.

Anyway, there was no need to conceal
something that nobody would want to steal.

'We 'ad wireless, and over the grate
yer gran kept souvenirs like a blue plate
from Rhyl, and that Scotty dog made of pot.
Before the war we didn't 'ave a lot.

"In the parlour we 'ad a three piece suite,
but that was for them walkin' down the street
and lookin' through the window, the way they
did. But we'd sit in there on Christmas Day.

"I can smell the cigar smoke now, and see
yer Dad and my Dad by the Christmas tree:
side by side on the settee sipping beer
and saying the things they said every year."

"I remember it well! Like a Sunday
except I wasn't allowed out to play.
More family than seats, locked in that small room
with fading daylight and increasing gloom."

"Can't say I remember you complainin'."
"Cold meat for tea with pickles and gherkin
followed by more mince-pies and marmalade.
A stomach full of wind from lemonade."

"Food was everywhere on Christmas Day;
and on the sideboard, yer gran put a tray
with a bowl of walnuts and bunch of grapes
and a packet of twenty Player's Weights."

"I remember those treats and sticky dates
packed like fresh faeces in small wooden crates;
the smell of gas from the spluttering fire,
and, in the background, the Bakelite choir."

"They were 'appy days, they were," Cathy sighed.
"Yer gran'd get dressed up, all dignified
in a black dress and she'd look a real treat
with lipstick and a touch of rouge on each cheek."

"And those thick-rimmed glasses she used to wear
with matching butterfly clip in her hair;
two balls of white wool on her slippered feet,
standing on a stool to carve the roast meat.

"Although yer gran was short, she was the boss:
when I was small, she'd take me across
'er knee. Mind, me dad 'ad't recovered
fully from the war and 'e discovered

"when 'e got 'ome from that 'ospital on
German soil, that 'is pre-war job 'ad gone.
The war 'ad been over two years by then
and 'e 'ad to start all over again.

"There was no work for the ex-servicemen,
and no benefits like today, and when
'e came 'ome after defending this land.
they gave 'im an 'ammer, nails and shoe-stand.

"But granddad wasn't a practical man:
'e wasn't much good with tools or oilcan;
and 'is 'ands were soft. More like the artist type.
That reminds me, I've got another gripe."

I had hoped she had forgotten the book,
but once again she had acquired the look
that incorporated a question-mark,
clarified by her following remark.

"And it isn't proper for a grandson
to write ' *gran lost all 'er teeth one by one*.
Me Mam's teeth came out in the dentist's chair,
just like my teeth did. And d'yer think it fair…"

END OF THE DAY

"The doctor called this morning; said 'e thinks
I should go in the Infirmary today.
Said 'e's worried about me 'eart and things.
I said no. At my age it'll be one-way."

Her voice was soft and breathless on the phone.

"The thought of going in drives me mad.
When they took yer gran, she didn't come 'ome;
and same with granddad and your mam and dad.
They must see you off when you're an OAP."

The ward was solemn and geriatric.

"Can't even get to the lav for a pee,
and the food's rubbish, it makes me feel sick.
How long do you think they'll keep me in for?
A few days? 'ave you told Joan and Alec? "

Like others names, these two were new to me.

"Come closer; I don't want that lot to 'ear.
Do you know the government's got the key
and they're going to lock us up in 'ere -
forever. It's true; you take it from me."

From lucidity to this in three day?

"There's a 'ole under this bed. Don't look now.
It leads down to a ground-floor alleyway
and the caf where they'll feed us. Anyhow,
When I see your mam I'll tell her you're okay."

My late mother died fifteen years ago.

"I 'aven't been on the toilet today.
They bring a commode in but I can't go
like that. It's too embarrassing that way.
I'll be all right if I don't eat or drink."

By the fourth day the prognosis was grave:
Cathy could neither recognize nor think,
and the nurse said she wouldn't last the day.
But it was the next day that she passed away.

I'm looking at her now: a beautiful,
young, blonde woman, her gaze returning mine
as she gently rebukes me out of that
sepia picture from 1939.

HARRY

The stroke had aged him in just a few days.
Once elegant, he slouched like a grey sack
in premature rigor mortis, but raised
a welcoming hand above his bent back.

By the fire, we sat in the dark'ning room.
He seemed to have forgotten I was there
and made waves with his good hand while entombed
behind a tartan blanket and fixed stare.

Unable now to link together thoughts,
this was a man who had mixed with royalty,
negotiated deals with several naughts,
but never lost sight of humility.

"Any old friends been to see you?" I asked.
He put a hand to his distorted face
and shook his head. Age and fate had unmasked
what awaits us all some time and place.

"How's business?" he asked, suddenly alert.
"And what's the dollar exchange rate today?
Don't use that so-called financial expert;
she phoned me when I was on holiday!"

With a gesture, he drew me to his side
and whispered: "How will I cope now mum's died?"
There was a look of real fear in his eyes,
and, for that thirty-year old death, he cried.

GEOFF

'*Dad's dead,*' I heard the voice on the phone say.
'*He thought he'd live forever and a day.*'
A misconception we shared, I replied,
his vivid image dancing in my mind.

Dead? The man who could talk for hours on Keynes.
Dead? Oxford! He who read for PhD.
Dead? All his mature learning come to that.
Dead? How will the pub fill the gap?

"*How's your Mum*?" I asked, after drinking air.
'*She's okay,*' she said. '*She's fine. Life goes on*'.
I heard the fingers running through her hair.
"*When*?" '*Yesterday,*' came the abstract reply.

Twenty-eight years of friendship down the line
since we first discussed the philosophies
of McCarthy, Karl Marx and Socrates,
church and Western industrial decline.

And the humanitarian principles
of time, place and space we occupied
in the nicotine and cataleptic bar
of braless barmaids and coughing catarrh.

We talked of Shakespeare and Renaissance man,
surrounded by narrow conversations
of prejudice and intimidation,
and blasphemy, sex and segregation.

Dead? He who dressed for comfort not disguise
and was looked down upon by lesser eyes,
by those who would never have an intellect
to compare if they lived a thousand years.

Dead? The man whose history I had shared
through the short seasons of a working life
of tar-macadam madness and routine,
of mortgage payments and God Save the Queen.

It was a grey day when the hearse passed by
on its quiet penultimate ride
along the road to wife and cold fireside.
I wondered if they had dressed him for town,

or in a gown – for a glass-sided hearse?
He would not have been seen dead in a skirt.
He'd prefer an old cardie and plaid shirt.
What was on his mind just before he died?

Perhaps a macroeconomic aspect
of the Keynesian intervention kind?
Or a pint of bitter beer by his side?
I had no cap or hat to raise in respect,

nothing tangible to express those years
of shared aspirations and life's concerns,
the balancing between nurture and work.
Goodbye, old boy, was his favourite phrase.

In a whisper, I reciprocated.

CLIVE

In a man-made forest we sat under a tree,
by the side of a track, in the rain, him and me.
And the rain clung to the pine needles the way my
companion clung to thought, under the lead-grey sky.
"*It's a very wet day*," I said, and he replied:
"*Yes, but look at the wonders of the countryside.*"
And together we watched a long-tailed bird walking
up an adjacent tree near where we sat talking.
"*That little mouse-like bird climbing the bark*," he said,
"*is called a treecreeper*," and he unwrapped his bread.
Side-by-side in the rain we ate our midday meal
and talked of what we saw, for only that was real.
The Alzheimer's disease, first seen three years before,
made spaces in his mind and was closing the door
on his short-term recall, while long-term implants like
chemical formulae were engraved on his psyche.
"*What day is it?*" he asked. "*Sunday*," I clarified.
"*They're all the same to me*," with a grin, he replied.
He studied the wrapping on his chocolate bar
but shook his head and then said: "*Did we walk far?*"
We had climbed a mountain
and then climbed down again.
